My Brother Is a Runner

Written by Jin-ha Gong
Illustrated by Hae-nam Park
Edited by Joy Cowley

big & SMALL

It is early in the morning.
Samuel wakes up and looks for his shoes.
Last week, his mother sold a goat
to buy him some new running shoes.
Samuel imagines himself at a training camp.
The thought makes him feel very excited.

In Kenya, many children want to be trained at a marathon
camp so they can become long-distance runners.

But then Samuel thinks of his sister Jubilee.
If he goes to marathon camp,
Jubilee will have to do all his chores.
Now he feels guilty.
He wakes his sister, and they walk
together in the chilly morning air.
Samuel decides to tell Jubilee how he feels.

"Jubilee, can you handle everything without me?" he asks. "It will be extra work for you."

"Don't worry, brother," she says. "Trust me!"

They work together, drawing water, collecting wood, setting the fire, and milking the cows. When Samuel is away, Jubilee will have to do all of this on her own.

The family gathers around to have breakfast.
They eat ugali, made from corn powder,
and warm milk.
Their stomachs grow full,
and they have more energy.
Mother offers Samuel some more ugali,
but he passes it on to Jubilee.

Tomorrow, Samuel has to leave home.
He packs his things in a bag.

"Can't you stay here?" says Jubilee.

Samuel replies, "If I become a great runner,
our family can live in a big house
and you can have nice clothes and shoes."

"Then I want to be a runner, too,"
Jubilee tells him.

"Jubilee, do you remember the animals
we saw in Nairobi National Park?
If you can pretend you are a cheetah
running after its prey, you will be
the fastest runner in the world."

"When you are tired, Jubilee,
walk slowly like the elephants.
They are big but they tread softly –
their feet make no sound at all.
By going slowly, you will get new strength
and you'll feel like running again."

"Jubilee, the zebras will show you
the right pace.
If you match your running feet
to the zebras' galloping beats,
you will cross the finish line
in no time at all."

Samuel says, "I will give you
my old pair of running shoes.
When you can run as fast as me,
I will buy you some new shoes."

Jubilee hugs her brother's shoes
and nods in silence.

Samuel waves to his family.
"So long, everybody! Goodbye, Jubilee!
Don't worry about me at marathon camp.
I will be a great runner one day."

Jubilee shouts,
"Brother, goodbye!
Hakuna matata!
Don't worry about me.
Good luck!"

25

About Kenya
A Country Where Nature and People Live Together

The Kenyan flag was created after they gained independence from the British in 1963. The black color represents the people and the red represents fighting for freedom. The green stands for agriculture and natural resources. The white bands represent unity and peace. The Maasai shield and spear in the middle represent the protection of freedom.

Children Who Dream of Becoming Marathon Runners

Kenya consists of mountain areas, coastal areas and plains. The high mountain areas have rich soil which means about three quarters of the Kenyan population live there. The Kenyan capital, Nairobi, is 5,577 feet (1,700 meters) above sea level. In higher areas, it can be hard to breathe because of the lack of oxygen. However, since Kenyans live in higher areas, they have greater lung function than people living at sea level. That is why many Kenyans can run long distances without losing their breath, and why Kenya has a reputation for being a nation of long-distance runners. Many children dream of winning marathons because it would bring them great wealth and honor.

Kenyan runners, Henry Kipkosgei and Stanley Salil competing in a marathon.

A Kenyan boy smiling while running

Hakuna Matata!

Jubilee said, "Hakuna matata!" to Samuel when he was leaving home. It is a commonly used phrase among Kenyans, and means "no worries."

Ugali, the Main Meal for Kenyans

Samuel's family ate ugali for breakfast. Ugali is a main meal in East African countries, including Kenya. It is made by cooking corn powder with water. They usually garnish ugali with meat and vegetables. Ugali is a staple food – like rice is for Asians and potatoes and bread for Europeans.

Ugali being made

Nairobi National Park

Nairobi National Park is near the Kenyan capital Nairobi. Established in 1946, it is Kenya's oldest national park. Although it isn't big, many animals live there, such as elephants, lions, and hippopotamuses.

A family of African bush elephants taking a mud bath in Tsavo East National Park, Kenya.

Children in the City

In Nairobi, there are many cars and tall modern buildings. It's a big city, and the children living there grow up in a wealthy environment. They go to school and wear uniforms. After school, they play with their friends.

Children studying computer science in Nairobi

Children in the Countryside

In the rural areas of Kenya, children have to help their parents from a young age. They have to fetch water, milk cows or goats and look after their younger brothers and sisters. Children walk long distances to schools that have very little equipment. Sometimes "school" is simply the shade under a tree.

In the country, even young children have to fetch water.

The Maasai People

The Maasai people live on the border of Tanzania and Kenya. Usually they live in tribal groups and raise livestock. They are tall and known for their nomadic lifestyle. Boys in their late teens become warriors and protect their livestock and their village. Sometimes they have to fight wild beasts that hunt their cattle, and retrieve stolen livestock from other tribes. Today, some Maasai people live in city areas.

Maasai children tending cattle

Lake Nakuru National Park, a Bird's Haven

The Lake Nakuru National Park is situated along Lake Nakuru in West Kenya. Lake Nakuru is the world's largest flamingo habitat. During peak season, over a million flamingos gather in Nakuru Lake. The lake is home to over 450 different species of birds.

A flock of flamingos in Lake Nakuru National Park

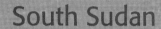

South Sudan

Democratic Republic of the Congo

Kenya

Name: Republic of Kenya

Location: East Africa

Area: 362,042 mi^2 (582,650 km^2)

Capital: Nairobi

Population: Approx. 44.35 million (2014)

Language: English, Swahili

Religion: Christianity (Catholic, Protestant), Islam

Main exports: Flowers, coffee, tea

Rwanda

Brundi

Lake Tanganyika

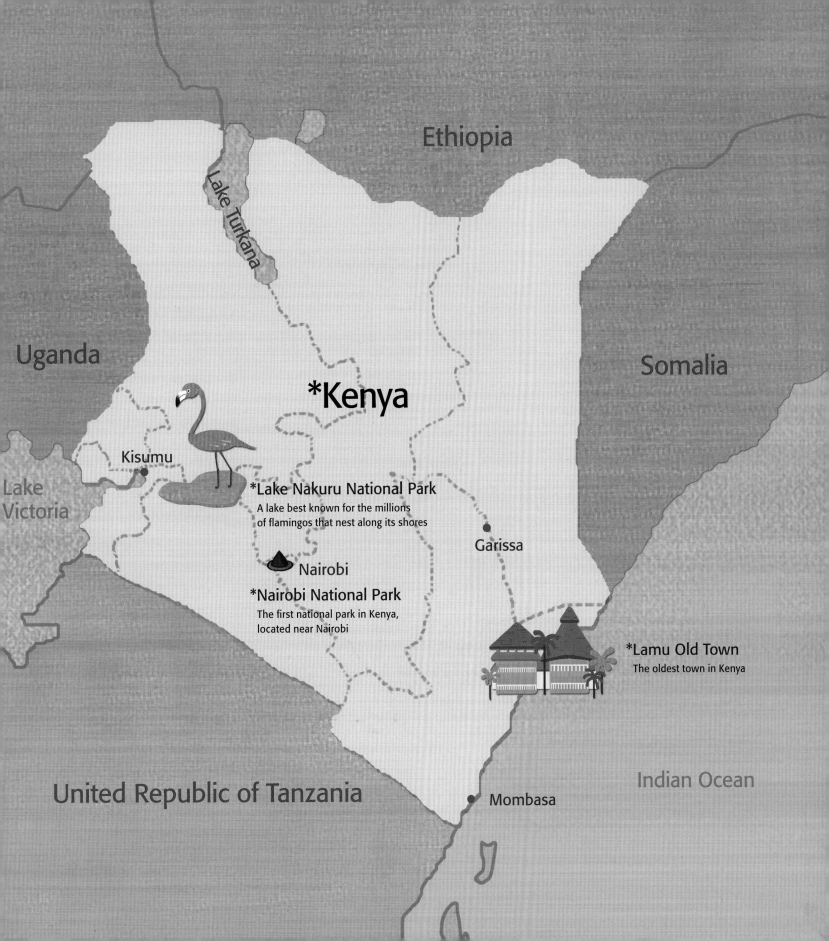

Ethiopia

Uganda

Lake Turkana

*Kenya

Somalia

Kisumu

Lake
Victoria

*Lake Nakuru National Park
A lake best known for the millions
of flamingos that nest along its shores

Garissa

Nairobi

*Nairobi National Park
The first national park in Kenya,
located near Nairobi

*Lamu Old Town
The oldest town in Kenya

United Republic of Tanzania

Mombasa

Indian Ocean

Original Korean text by Jin-ha Gong
Illustrations by Hae-nam Park
Korean edition © Aram Publishing

This English edition published by big & SMALL in 2016
by arrangement with Aram Publishing
English text edited by Joy Cowley
English edition © big & SMALL 2016

Distributed in the United States and Canada by
Lerner Publishing Group, Inc.
241 First Avenue North
Minneapolis, MN 55401 U.S.A.
www.lernerbooks.com

Images by page no. - left to right, top to bottom
Page 26: © Christian Jansky (CC-BY-SA-3.0); Erik (HASH) Hersman (CC-BY-2.0);
Page 27: public domain; public domain; © I, Mgiganteus (GFDL);
Page 28: © Stephen wanjau (CC-BY-SA-3.0); © Daryona (CC-BY-SA-3.0);
Page 29: © Georgio (CC-BY-1.0); © Paul Mannix (CC-BY-SA-2.0)

ISBN: 978-1-925247-52-7

Printed in Korea